GHOSTS

MARYSA STORM

BLACK RABBIT BOOKS

Bolt Jr. is published by Black Rabbit Books
P.O. Box 3263, Mankato, Minnesota, 56002.
www.blackrabbitbooks.com
Copyright © 2020 Black Rabbit Books

Grant Gould, designer; Omay Ayres, photo researcher

Names: Storm, Marysa, author.
Title: Ghosts / Marysa Storm.
Description: Mankato, MN : Black Rabbit Books, 2020. |
Series: Bolt Jr. A little bit spooky | Includes bibliographical
references and index. Identifiers: LCCN 2018057354 (print) |
LCCN 2019007326 (ebook) | ISBN 9781623101824 (ebook)
| ISBN 9781623101763 (library binding) |
ISBN 9781644661147 (paperback)
Subjects: LCSH: Ghosts–Juvenile literature.
Classification: LCC BF1461 (ebook) | LCC BF1461 .S876
2020 (print) | DDC 133.1–dc23
LC record available at https://lccn.loc.gov/2018057354

Printed in the United States. 5/19

Image Credits

Alamy: Chronicle, 5; Dale O'Dell, 10–11; Dreamstime: Katalinks,
20–21; Topgeek, Cover (ghost); mrps.org: The Ohio State
Reformatory, 16–17; Science Source: Ian Hooton, 12–13;
Shutterstock: Bodor Tivadar, 14; EvilWata, 7; Fer Gregory, 1;
Fernando Cortes, 18 (bkgd); Hollygraphic, 8–9; jordeangjelovik,
18 (camera); Linda Bucklin, 18; Ilaszlo, Cover (bkgd); mipan,
18 (thermometer); Nadiia Kalameiets, 6; robuart, 3, 24; Sandra
Cunningham, 22–23; Tartila, 13; Valentyna7, 18 (recorder);
Vectorpocket, 4, 10, 21; Stocksy: Rachel Bellinsky, 6–7

Contents

CHAPTER 1

A Scary Story

It was a normal night for the Bell family. But then a **strange** noise began. It sounded like someone hitting the house. John Bell ran outside. But no one was there. Was it a ghost?

strange: different from what is usual, normal, or expected

COMPARING BELIEVERS

About 58% of Americans don't believe in ghosts.

Super Spooky

People tell many ghost stories.
They say ghosts haunt places. Some
people believe their stories. Others say
they're all made-up.

▶ **About 42%
of Americans**
believe in ghosts.

POSSIBLE SIGNS OF A

Ghost

strange noises

cold spots

disappearing figures

weird lights

CHAPTER 2

Strange Happenings

Stories describe ghosts in different ways. Some say ghosts look like real people. Others say they're **see-through**. In some stories, ghosts appear as lights.

see-through: thin enough to be seen through

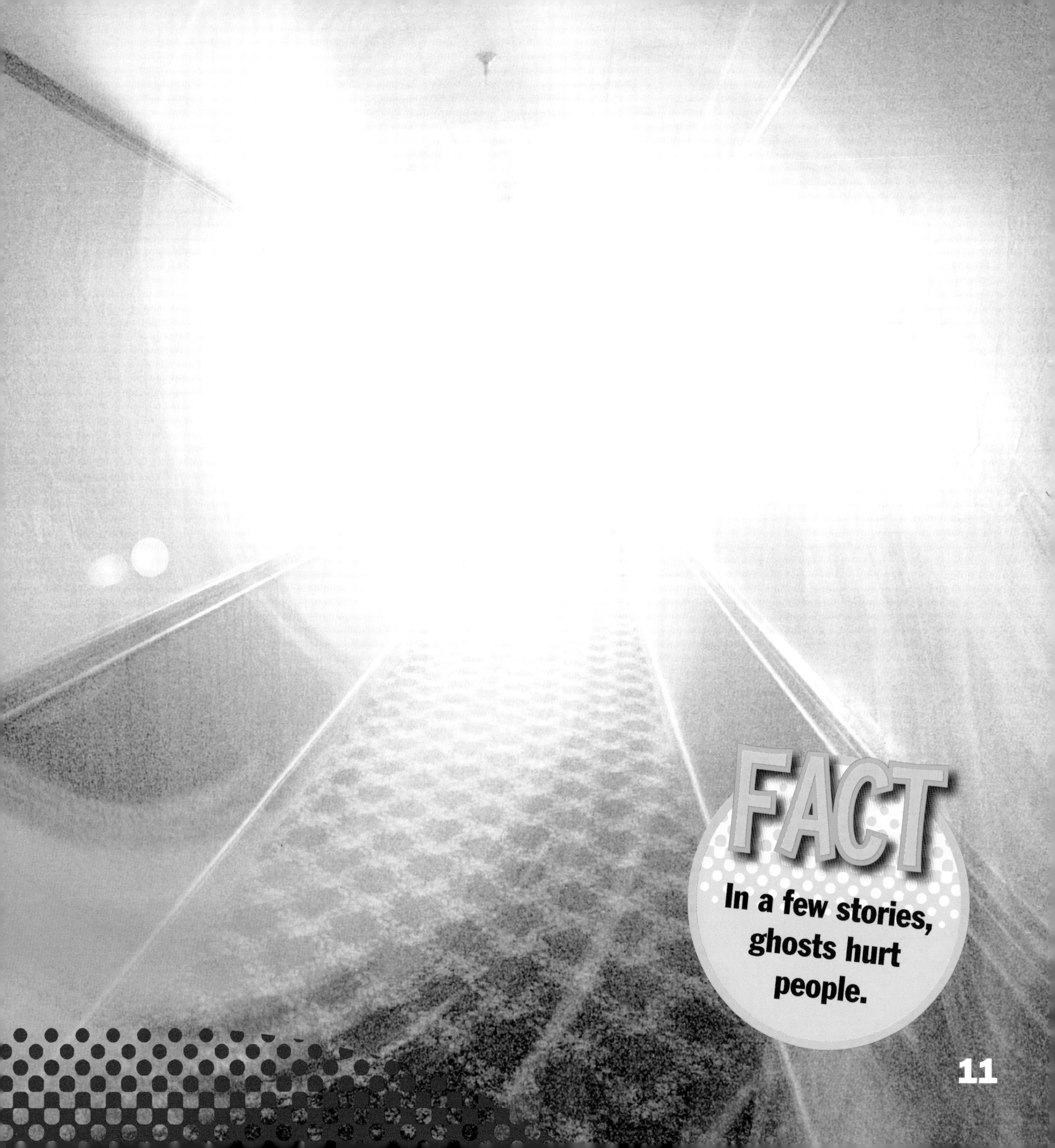

FACT

In a few stories, ghosts hurt people.

How They Act

Not all ghosts act the same way. Some stories say they make noises. They might **knock** on walls. Other stories say ghosts move objects. They cause cold spots.

knock: to hit something

Ghost Stories around the World

United States
People tell of ghosts where battles happened.

England
People talk of a royal ghost.

Sweden
Some say there's a train of ghosts.

CHAPTER 3

Studying the Stories

Ghost hunters search for ghosts. They look for proof. They go places people say are haunted. They take pictures and watch for lights.

FACT

Ghost stories come from all around the world.

video camera **recorder** **thermometer**

The Real Reason?

Most stories have simple
explanations. Animals could be
making the noises. Old windows
could let cold air in.

But some stories are harder
to explain. Could ghosts be real?

. . . . **Tools Used to Hunt Ghosts**

Bonus Facts

Some people think ghosts can cause smells.

People **believe** ghosts haunt battle sites.

Ghost stories go back thousands of years.

People say the White House has ghosts.

White House: where U.S. presidents live

READ MORE/WEBSITES

Giannini, Alex. *Frightening Farmhouses.* Scary Places. New York: Bearport Publishing Company, Inc., 2019.

Oachs, Emily Rose. *Ghosts.* Investigating the Unexplained. Minneapolis: Bellwether Media, Inc., 2019.

Troupe, Thomas Kingsley. *Extreme Ghost Stories.* That's Just Spooky! Mankato, MN: Black Rabbit Books, 2019.

7 Spooky Things You Didn't Know about Ghosts
www.cbc.ca/kidscbc2/the-feed/monsters-101-all-about-ghosts

Ghosts
sd4kids.skepdic.com/ghosts.html

Introduction to Ghost Investigating
kids.ghostvillage.com/jrghosthunters/index.shtml

GLOSSARY

knock (NOK)—to hit something

see-through (SEE-throo)—thin enough to be seen through

strange (STREYNJ)—different from what is usual, normal, or expected

White House (WAHYT HOUS)—where U.S. presidents live

INDEX